REBEL GIRLS

Little Library

10+ Women who Make Music

This is a work of creative nonfiction. It is a collection of heartwarming and thought-provoking stories inspired by the lives and adventures of influential women. It is not an encyclopedic account of the events and accomplishments of their lives.

www.rebelgirls.com

Rebel Girls, Inc.
421 Elm Ave.
Larkspur, CA 94939

Text by Dinah Dunn
Art direction by Giulia Flamini
Graphic design by Kristen Brittain
Graphic design and additional illustrations: Alessandro Raimondo
Portrait illustrations: 4: Eline Van Dam, 8: Emma Eubanks,
12: Kamo Frank, 16: Cari Vander Yacht, 20: Keisha Okafor,
24: Sharee Miller, 28: Tamiki, 32: Eugenia Mello,
36: Anna Dixoni, 40: Rafaela Rijo-Núñez

Printed in China, 2023
10 9 8 7 6 5 4 3 2 1
ISBN: 979-8-88964-074-5

FSC
www.fsc.org
MIX
Paper | Supporting responsible forestry
FSC™ C018179

CONTENTS

Beyoncé

Singer, Songwriter, and Businesswoman

Born September 4, 1981 | USA

Beyoncé stood backstage with her singing group. They were about to compete on a TV show called *Star Search*. She was more excited than nervous. *We can do this*, she thought.

Her group had been practicing after school, on weekends, and during summer vacations. They were better than ever. The judges *had* to see that.

Finally, it was their turn! Beyoncé and the other girls sang and danced their hearts out. When they finished, they knew they had done their best.

Beyoncé crossed her fingers as the judges made their choice. But when the winner was announced, it wasn't their group. They lost? The girls hugged each other and cried.

And the next day, they went back to work. They weren't giving up.

When she was 17, Beyoncé wrote the first big song for the group, now named Destiny's Child. It was the first of many hits. Their records won three Grammys, America's biggest music award. People all over the world loved their music.

Beyoncé was a star, but she still wanted more. When the group stopped performing together, she kept working. She put out an album of her own songs. Beyoncé was proud of the music because she had tried something new.

Beyoncé continued to work and grow. She put out six more albums, which sold millions of copies. She used her music and money to support the rights of women, Black people, and the LGBTQIA+ community. She sang at the Super Bowl halftime show twice. She designed clothes with her mom. She acted in movies. And by 2023, she had won more Grammy Awards than anyone in history.

Beyoncé's hard work has taken her further than she ever dreamed. No wonder she is an inspiration for people around the world.

SCAN TO HEAR MORE!

K-Pop Band

Formed in 2016 | South Korea, New Zealand, and Thailand

Once there was a little girl named Rosé who loved to play guitar and sing songs by her favorite artists. When she was 16, her dad heard that a South Korean music company was putting together a girl group. They were looking for girls in lots of places—even where Rosé lived in Australia!

Rosé jumped at the chance to try out. And she made the cut! She flew thousands of miles to join Jisoo, Jennie, and Lisa in South Korea. When they met, it was like they had always been friends. "We just clicked," said Rosé. They stayed up all night singing together.

There they trained together for years to become the pop group

Blackpink. For 12 hours a day, seven days a week, they practiced singing and dancing. It was really difficult. Sometimes Rosé would call her parents crying. But the hard work just made her want to do better.

All their practice paid off. Their first single, "Boombayah," a bouncy party song, reached number one on the charts. And that was just the beginning of their success. Song after song became popular all over the world. People loved Blackpink's cool fashion choices and dance moves. Their videos got more than a billion views on YouTube.

In 2023, Blackpink made history again. They were the main

performers at the popular American music festival Coachella. They were the first K-pop girl group to do that!

What makes them so successful? Each member adds something to the mix. Jennie loves fashion and her focus keeps the group on track. Jisoo is the oldest and makes sure everyone is okay before big performances. Rosé's sweet voice fills the songs with feeling. Lisa's playful rapping and amazing dance moves have the girls smiling even on tough days.

Their hard work has made them more like sisters than friends.

SCAN TO HEAR MORE!

DJ Switch Ghana

DJ

Born December 12, 2007 | Ghana and USA

On the west coast of Africa, in the country of Ghana, there lived a girl whose superpower was making people happy. Her name was Erica, but on stage spinning records, dancing, rapping, and singing, she used a special name.

"I picked the name DJ Switch because when I was a kid I was switching up the mood of people. When you're sad, I'll make you happy!" she said with a great big grin.

When she was nine years old, her parents hired a DJ to train Erica. He taught her how to use turntables and mix songs. She loved it!

Soon Erica was competing on a talent show on TV. "I was not feeling shy," she said, "and I wanted to give it my best." She won! The next year she was the youngest person ever to win Ghana's biggest DJ competition.

Since then, she has performed on stages all over the world. She was invited to New York City to make music with the Grammy-winning artist Wyclef Jean. Millions of people have also watched her show off her skills online.

Erica has learned a lot along the way. She has some tips for success as a DJ: 1. Practice. 2. Love music. 3. Be excited. 4. Take it seriously. And 5. Have a positive attitude.

In 2022, she made another big

switch. She moved to the United States to go to high school. She hopes it will bring her a step closer to her other dream: being a doctor who delivers babies.

How does she plan on balancing the two? “Let’s say in the future you come to my hospital and you want to deliver,” she says. “I’ll just be playing some music and you’ll see your baby dancing while it’s coming!”

Joan Jett

Rock Star

Born September 22, 1958 | USA

Joan loved rock 'n' roll. One Christmas, when she was 13 years old, she got her first guitar. She was thrilled—but something was missing. Playing on her own was okay, she thought. *But if I really want to be a rock star, I need a band.*

Two years later, she had her band together: Sandy on drums, Cherie on vocals, Jackie on bass, and Lita on lead guitar. With Joan on rhythm guitar and singing, they were . . . the Runaways.

They were 16 but they played everywhere, even clubs for adults.

You're too young, people said.

So what? they shouted back.

You're too loud, people complained.

They just played louder.

Girls can't be punk rockers, people told them.

Oh yeah? Just watch us!

"We didn't want barriers put up on what we were allowed to sing about, say, or play," said Joan. One of their first songs, "Cherry Bomb," was a smash. Their second album, *Queens of Noise*, became a hit in countries around the world.

It wasn't always easy, though. Back home, they traveled to shows in a beat-up old van, driving from town to town through the night. Onstage, sometimes people would shout at them or throw things. But the Runaways didn't care.

They lived for the music.

After years, the touring life became too hard. Some of the band quit. So Joan went out on her own. Her first album was called *I Love Rock 'n' Roll*. It sold more than 10 million copies! And Joan kept playing and was inducted into the Rock and Roll Hall of Fame.

Nearly 50 years later, Joan is still rocking out. Her advice for girls who are told they are too loud or shouldn't rock? "You have to fight for your own self. No one is going to give it to you."

SCAN TO HEAR MORE!

MC Soffia

Rapper

Born February 22, 2004 | Brazil

Soffia's greatest power is her voice. She uses it to send a very important message: may Black girls love and accept themselves and each other.

When Soffia was just five years old, her classmates began bullying her because of her dark skin. They said terrible things to Soffia. Their words hurt her.

I want to be white, Soffia told her mother.

Kamilah, her mom, was upset. She knew being Black was beautiful and powerful. There was absolutely nothing wrong with Soffia's dark skin. So Kamilah began teaching her to love herself.

When Soffia was six years old, she went to her first hip-hop workshop. She fell in love with rapping. She said, “I wanted to make rap music because it helps you say how you are feeling, what you’re seeing, and what is happening.” She worked on lyrics that would later be recorded in a real studio.

In 2016, she released her first music video. The song was called “Menina Pretinha,” which means “little Black girl” in Portuguese. In it, 12-year-old Soffia sang: “I’m Black, and I’m proud of my color.”

That same year, Soffia performed with the most famous female rapper in Brazil, Karol Conká. It was the opening ceremony of the Rio Olympics. The whole world was watching them.

Backstage, Soffia was nervous. But when she held the microphone in her hand, she knew she was ready. She stepped onto the enormous stage. Her words flowed out with power.

Soffia knew she was there for all the Black kids who weren't on stage with her. "I'll be their voice," she said.

Nandi Bushell

Drummer

Born April 28, 2010 | South Africa and UK

Once there was a girl who spread joy and happiness one beat at a time. Nandi was born in Durban, South Africa. Her family moved to England when she was two years old.

When Nandi was five, her father would play music from the British rock band the Beatles while making her pancakes. She loved the way the drummer, Ringo Starr, played. She wanted to be like him!

Her parents said she could have a drum kit if she did well in school. So Nandi did her schoolwork and got good grades. Soon she had a drum kit of her own.

Nandi's father started teaching her how to play her new drums. She practiced every day, and soon enough, she was playing better than him! Nandi loved rock music. She could copy all her favorite songs.

Her parents saw how talented she was. They recorded her playing the drums and guitar and posted the videos on social media. They went viral! Even famous rock stars found out about her.

One of these rock stars, Lenny Kravitz, was so impressed he invited Nandi to play with him in London. She was thrilled! Lenny was one of her favorite musicians.

Nandi also got into an online rock battle with the famous drummer

Dave Grohl. They challenged each other to play songs. After a few songs, he said that she won. He then invited her to play with his band, Foo Fighters. He was knocked out by Nandi's love of the music. He said, "If that doesn't inspire you, I don't know what will."

Nandi also writes her own songs. When her dad was dealing with depression, she wrote a song that described how he felt called "The Shadows." It made her dad very proud.

SCAN TO HEAR MORE!

Renata Flores

Singer-Songwriter

Born March 20, 2001 | Peru

Once upon a time in Ayacucho, Peru, there lived a girl named Renata. She grew up surrounded by tall mountains that touched the clouds. Her people were Indigenous tribes who had lived there for thousands of years.

Renata listened to her grandparents talk in a language she couldn't understand. The language was known as Quechua, or Runasimi. Millions of people speak it, but older people often don't teach it to their kids. They don't want their children to get made fun of for speaking an old language.

Renata wanted to be connected to her history. She decided to learn Quechua. Renata's grandmothers helped, teaching her how to say words correctly. She also took language classes. Soon she wasn't just speaking in Quechua, she was singing! And she had a wonderful idea. Maybe the way to help save the language was through music.

Renata was 14 when she filmed herself singing "The Way You Make Me Feel" by Michael Jackson. But she sang all of the lyrics in Quechua. Millions of people watched the video, knocked out by Renata's singing voice. The beauty of the music made many people interested in learning the language.

Renata now releases her own songs. Like a bridge from the past to the future, the songs talk about the history of her Indigenous people. She wears clothing from her culture in her music videos. “I want to be the voice of those people who are unheard and forgotten,” she says. And she’s doing it one song at a time.

Selena Quintanilla Pérez

Tejano Singer

April 16, 1971–March 31, 1995 | USA

Selena was nine when she formed a band with her brothers and sisters. They were called Selena y Los Dinos. Selena had a beautiful voice, so she became the singer. They practiced every day. Soon they began playing to small audiences in their home state of Texas.

Life was tough for Selena's family. They lost their home because they didn't have enough money. Selena y Los Dinos wasn't doing well until the band started playing Tejano. Tejano is Mexican American music filled with emotion.

Some people thought Selena shouldn't be singing Tejano music. It was usually sung by men. She didn't let that stop her. "When I am singing,

I am a completely different person. I could be very free," she said. "I could do what I want."

Eventually, Selena went out on her own. Her concerts began drawing crowds of thousands. She won a Grammy Award for best Mexican/American album. When Selena heard, she couldn't believe it! But whether she believed it or not, Selena was becoming a star.

In 1995, Selena performed at the Houston Astrodome to an audience of 61,000 people. She wore a sparkly purple jumpsuit. Selena's smile

spread from ear to ear as she looked out at the crowd.

"Manos arriba!" Selena shouted as the music began. The crowd did as they were told. They lifted their hands in the air, dancing and singing along with her.

Sadly, this amazing show would be Selena's last performance.

"If you have a dream," Selena once said, "don't let anyone take it away." Selena realized many of her own dreams, but not all of them. She died when she was 23. But her lovely music lives on.

SCAN TO HEAR MORE!

Taylor Swift

Singer-Songwriter

Born December 13, 1989 | USA

From the time she was 12 years old, Taylor would play the guitar for hours. She was going through a hard time at school and didn't have many friends. The music helped her get through those difficult years.

Taylor put her feelings into her song lyrics. Then she dreamed up melodies to match. And when her fingers bled, she would tape them up and keep playing.

Taylor wanted to become a country music star, so her family moved from Pennsylvania to Nashville, Tennessee. In Nashville, the home of country music, she played on any stage she could find. She asked everyone to call radio stations and request her songs. Soon people noticed her talent. *Who is this young girl with the golden curls?* they wondered.

At 16, Taylor got a record deal. She couldn't wait to put out her first album. When she did, it was a hit! She became the youngest person to write and sing a number one song. She was also the youngest to win a Grammy Award for album of the year.

It was only the first of many award-winning albums. Fans everywhere love her songs. They help people get through hard times—just like they helped Taylor when she was young.

Taylor has become one of the most powerful women in the music business. She stands up for women and people in the LGBTQIA+ community. In 2018, she reached out to her hundreds of millions of followers to get them out to vote.

No matter how famous she gets, Taylor knows how important it is to be kind. "No matter what happens in life, be good to people," she says.

SCAN TO HEAR MORE!

Temilayo Abodunrin

Saxophonist

Born November 19, 2009 | Nigeria

Temilayo was playing instruments when most kids were playing with blocks. By the time she was four years old, she could already play the keyboard.

One day, she went to a church concert. The saxophonist stepped forward and began to play. Temilayo couldn't look away. The beautiful sound, the shiny gold color—this instrument was amazing! *I want to try that*, Temilayo thought.

Temilayo begged her parents for a sax. Soon they got her one. For Temilayo, weekdays were for school, but weekends were for music. Nothing could keep her from her sax!

Temilayo learned quickly. Before long she was playing her new instrument at weddings while brides and grooms danced under sparkly lights. She played at churches where people clapped to her music between preaching.

Because she was so young, the audience expected her to play simple songs. Instead, she played difficult tunes beautifully. Temilayo tried not to let other people make her doubt herself. She started posting videos of her own versions of popular songs.

Church services and weddings soon turned into bigger concerts. Temilayo shared the stage with famous Nigerian artists like Johnny Drille, Wole Oni, and Davido. In 2020, she recorded "Ayo," a song she'd written. The video for "Ayo" shows her wearing colorful clothes, grooving to the beat.

Temilayo followed her love of the saxophone. It led her to amazing opportunities, all because she was brave enough to try something new.

About Rebel Girls

Rebel Girls is a global, multi-platform empowerment brand dedicated to helping raise the most inspired and confident generation of girls through content, experiences, products, and community. Originating from an international best-selling children's book, Rebel Girls amplifies stories of real-life women throughout history, geography, and field of excellence. With a growing community of nearly 20 million self-identified Rebel Girls spanning more than 100 countries, the brand engages with Generation Alpha through its book series, award-winning podcast, events, and merchandise. With the 2021 launch of the Rebel Girls app, the company has created a flagship destination for girls to explore a wondrous world filled with inspiring true stories of extraordinary women.

As a B Corp, we're part of a global community of businesses that meet high standards of social and environmental impact.

Join the Rebel Girls community:

Facebook: facebook.com/rebelgirls
Instagram: @rebelgirls
Twitter: @rebelgirlsbook
TikTok: @rebelgirlsbook
Web: rebelgirls.com
Podcast: rebelgirls.com/podcast
App: rebelgirls.com/audio

If you liked this book, please take a moment to review it wherever you prefer!